The Old Huntsman & Other Poems by Siegfried Sassoon

Siegfried Loraine Sassoon was born on 8th September 1886.

Sassoon was educated at the New Beacon School, Sevenoaks, Kent then Marlborough College, Wiltshire and finally at Clare College, Cambridge, where from 1905 to 1907 he read history. He went down from Cambridge without a degree and spent the next few years indulging himself hunting, playing cricket and writing verse.

However, motivated by patriotism, Sassoon joined the Sussex Yeomanry of the British Army as the threat of war escalated into open conflict.

His early poems exhibit a Romantic, dilettantish sweetness but his war poetry moves to an increasingly discordant beat, stridently conveying the ugly truths of the trenches to an audience hitherto placated by jingoistic and patriotic propaganda.

Sassoon's periods of duty on the Western Front were marked by near-suicidal missions, including the single-handed capture of a German trench. Armed with grenades, he scattered sixty German soldiers.

In 1919 took up a post as literary editor of the socialist Daily Herald. Here he was responsible for employing several eminent reviewers, including E. M. Forster and Charlotte Mew. Sassoon also commissioned new material from the likes of Arnold Bennett and Osbert Sitwell.

Sassoon was now, in 1928, preparing to take a new direction by branching out into prose, with 'Memoirs of a Fox-Hunting Man'. This anonymously published first volume of a fictionalised autobiography, was acclaimed as a classic, bringing its author fame as a humorous writer. Other volumes including his own autobiography based on his youth and early manhood across three volumes followed.

In his last years Sassoon converted to Roman Catholicism and was admitted to the faith at Downside Abbey in Somerset.

Siegfried Loraine Sassoon, CBE, MC died from stomach cancer on 1st September 1967, a week before his 81st birthday.

Index of Contents

To THOMAS HARDY, O.M.

The Old Huntsman

[To Norman Loder]

I've never ceased to curse the day I signed
A seven years' bargain for the Golden Fleece.
'Twas a bad deal all round; and dear enough
It cost me, what with my daft management,
And the mean folk as owed and never paid me,
And backing losers; and the local bucks
Egging me on with whiskies while I bragged
The man I was when huntsman to the Squire.

I'd have been prosperous if I'd took a farm
Of seventy acres, drove my gig and haggled
At Monday markets; now I've squandered all
My savings; nigh three hundred pound I got
As testimonial when I'd grown too stiff
And slow to press a beaten fox.

      The Fleece!
'Twas the damned Fleece that wore my Emily out,
The wife of thirty years who served me well;
(Not like this beldam clattering in the kitchen.
That never trims a lamp nor sweeps the floor,
And brings me greasy soup in a foul crock.)

Blast the old harridan! What's fetched her now,
Leaving me in the dark, and short of fire?

And Where's my pipe? 'Tis lucky I've a turn
For thinking, and remembering all that's past.
And now's my hour, before I hobble to bed,
To set the works a-wheezing, wind the clock
That keeps the time of life with feeble tick
Behind my bleared old face that stares and wonders.

It's queer how, in the dark, comes back to mind
Some morning of September. We've been digging
In a steep, sandy warren, riddled with holes,
And I've just pulled the terrier out and left
A sharp-nosed cub-face Winking there and snapping,
Then in a moment seen him mobbed and torn
To strips in the baying hurly of the pack.
I picture it so clear: the dusty sunshine
On bracken, and the men with spades, that wipe
Red faces: one tilts up a mug of ale.
And, having stooped to clean my gory hands,
I whistle the jostling beauties out o' the wood.

I'm but a daft old fool! I often wish
The Squire were back again — ah, he was a man!
They don't breed men like him these days; he'd come
For sure, and sit and talk and suck his briar
Till the old wife brings up a dish of tea.

Ay, those were days, when I was serving Squire!
I never knowed such sport as '85,
The winter afore the one that snowed us silly.

Once in a way the parson will drop in
And read a bit o' the Bible, if I'm bad, —
Pray the Good Lord to make my spirit whole
In faith: he leaves some 'baccy on the shelf,
And wonders I don't keep a dog to cheer me,
Because he knows I'm mortal fond of dogs!

I ask you, what's a gent like that to me,
As wouldn't know Elijah if I saw him,
Nor have the wit to keep him on the talk?
'Tis kind of parson to be troubling still
With such as me; but he's a town-bred chap,
Full of his college notions and Christmas hymns.

Religion beats me. I'm amazed at folk
Drinking the gospels in and never scratching
Their heads for questions. When I was a lad
I learned a bit from mother, and never thought

To educate myself for prayers and psalms.

But now I'm old and bald and serious-minded,
With days to sit and ponder. I'd no chance
When young and gay to get the hang of all
This Hell and Heaven: and when the clergy hoick
And holloa from their pulpits, I'm asleep,
However hard I listen; and when they pray
It seems we're all like children sucking sweets
In school, and wondering whether master sees.

I used to dream of Hell when I was first
Promoted to a huntsman's job, and scent
Was rotten, and all the foxes disappeared,
And hounds were short of blood; and officers
From barracks over-rode 'em all day long
On weedy, whistling nags that knocked a hole
In every fence; good sportsmen to a man
And brigadiers by now, but dreadful hard
On a young huntsman keen to show some sport.

Ay, Hell was thick with captains, and I rode
The lumbering brute that's beat in half a mile.
And blunders into every blind old ditch.
Hell was the coldest scenting land I've known.
And both my whips were always lost, and hounds
Would never get their heads down; and a man
On a great yawing chesnut trying to cast 'em
While I was in a corner pounded by
The ugliest hog-backed stile you've clapped your eyes on.

There was an iron-spiked fence round all the coverts,
And civil-spoken keepers I couldn't trust,
And the main earth unstopp'd. The fox I found
Was always a three-legged 'un from a bag
Who reeked of aniseed and wouldn't run.
The farmers were all ploughing their old pasture
And bellowing at me when I rode their beans
To cast for beaten fox, or galloped on
With hounds to a lucky view. I'd lost my voice
Although I shouted fit to burst my guts,
And couldn't blow my horn.

            And when I woke,
Emily snored, and barn-cocks started crowing.
And morn was at the window; and I was glad
To be alive because I heard the cry
Of hounds like church-bells chiming on a Sunday, —

Ay, that's the song I'd wish to hear in Heaven!
The cry of hounds was Heaven for me: I know
Parson would call me crazed and wrong to say it,
But where's the use of life and being glad
If God's not in your gladness?

        I've no brains
For book-learned studies; but I've heard men say
There's much in print that clergy have to wink at:
Though many I've met were jolly chaps, and rode
To hounds, and walked me puppies; and could pick
Good legs and loins and necks and shoulders, ay,
And feet, — 'twas necks and feet I looked at first.

Some hounds I've known were wise as half your saints,
And better hunters. That old dog of the Duke's,
Harlequin; what a dog he was to draw!
And what a note he had, and what a nose
When foxes ran down wind and scent was catchy!
And that light lemon bitch of the Squire's, old Dorcas, —
She were a marvellous hunter, were old Dorcas!

Ay, oft I've thought: "If there were hounds in Heaven,
"With God as Master, taking no subscription;
"And all His blessed country farmed by tenants;
"And a straight-necked old fox in every gorse!"
But when I came to work it out, I found
There'd be too many huntsmen wanting places, —
Though some I've known might get a job with Nick!

I've come to think of God as something like
The figure of a man the old Duke was
When I was turning hounds to Nimrod King,
Before his Grace was took so bad with gout.
And had to quit the saddle. Tall and spare.
Clean-shaved and grey, with shrewd, kind eyes, that twinkled.

And easy walk; who, when he gave good words,
Gave them whole-hearted; and would never blame
Without just cause. Lord God might be like that.
Sitting alone in a great room of books
Some evening after hunting.

        Now I'm tired
With hearkening to the tick-tack on the shelf;
And pondering makes me doubtful.

        Riding home

On a moonless night of cloud that feels like frost
Though stars are hidden, (hold your feet up, horse!)
And thinking what a task I had to draw
A pack with all those lame 'uns, and the lot
Wanting a rest from all this open weather, —
That's what I'm doing now.

      And likely, too.
The frost'll be a long 'un, and the night
One sleep. The parsons say we'll wake to find
A country blinding-white with dazzle of snow.

The naked stars make men feel lonely, — wheeling
And glinting on the puddles in the road.
And then you listen to the wind, and wonder
If folk are quite such bucks as they appear
When dressed by London tailors, looking down
Their boots at covert side, and thinking big.

This world's a funny place to live in. Soon
I'll need to change my country; but I know
'Tis little enough I've understood my life,
And a power of sights I've missed, and foreign marvels.

I used to feel it, riding on spring days
In meadows pied with sun and chasing clouds.
And half forget how I was there to catch
The foxes; lose the angry, eager feeling
A huntsman ought to have, that's out for blood.
And means his hounds to get it!

      Now I know
It's God that speaks to us when we're bewitched.
Smelling the hay in June and smiling quiet;
Or when there's been a spell of summer drought.
Lying awake and listening to the rain.

I'd like to be the simpleton I was
In the old days when I was whipping-in
To a little harrier-pack in Worcestershire,
And loved a dairymaid, but never knew it
Until she'd wed another. So I've loved
My life; and when the good years are gone down.
Discover what I've lost.

      I never broke
Out of my blundering self into the world.
But let it all go past me, like a man

Half-asleep in a land that's full of wars.

What a grand thing 'twould be if I could go
Back to the kennels now and take my hounds
For summer exercise; be riding out
With forty couple when the quiet skies
Are streaked with sunrise, and the silly birds
Grown hoarse with singing; cobwebs on the furze
Up on the hill, and all the country strange,
With no one stirring; and the horses fresh.
Sniffing the air I'll never breathe again.

You've brought the lamp then, Martha? I've no mind
For newspaper to-night, nor bread and cheese.
Give me the candle, and I'll get to bed.

Absolution

The anguish of the earth absolves our eyes
Till beauty shines in all that we can see.
War is our scourge; yet war has made us wise,
And, fighting for our freedom, we are free.

Horror of wounds and anger at the foe,
And loss of things desired; all these must pass.
We are the happy legion, for we know
Time's but a golden wind that shakes the grass.

There was an hour when we were loth to part
From life we longed to share no less than others.
Now, having claimed this heritage of heart.
What need we more, my comrades and my brothers?

Brothers

Give me your hand, my brother, search my face;
Look in these eyes lest I should think of shame.
For we have made an end of all things base;
We are returning by the road we came.

Your lot is with the ghosts of soldiers dead,
And I am in the field where men must fight.
But in the gloom I see your laurell'd head
And through your victory I shall win the light.

The Dragon and the Undying

All night the flares go up; the Dragon sings
And beats upon the dark with furious wings;
And, stung to rage by his own darting fires,
Reaches with grappling coils from town to town;
He lusts to break the loveliness of spires,
And hurls their martyred music toppling down.

Yet, though the slain are homeless as the breeze.
Vocal are they, like storm-bewilder'd seas.
Their faces are the fair, unshrouded night,
And planets are their eyes, their ageless dreams.
Tenderly stooping earthward from their height,
They wander in the dusk with chanting streams;
And they are dawn-lit trees, with arms up-flung.
To hail the burning heavens they left unsung.

France

She triumphs, in the vivid green
Where sun and quivering foliage meet;
And in each soldier's heart serene;
When death stood near them they have seen
The radiant forests where her feet
Move on a breeze of silver sheen.

And they are fortunate, who fight
For gleaming landscapes swept and shafted
And crowned by cloud pavilions white;
Hearing such harmonies as might
Only from Heaven be downward wafted —
Voices of victory and delight.

To Victory

[To Edmund Gosse]

Return to greet me, colours that were my joy,
Not in the woeful crimson of men slain.
But shining as a garden; come with the streaming

Banners of dawn and sundown after rain.
I want to fill my gaze with blue and silver.
Radiance through living roses, spires of green
Rising in young-limbed copse and lovely wood
Where the hueless wind passes and cries unseen.

I am not sad; only I long for lustre, —
Tired of the greys and browns and the leafless ash.
I would have hours that move like a glitter of dancers
Far from the angry guns that boom and flash.
Return, musical, gay with blossom and fleetness,
Days when my sight shall be clear and my heart rejoice;
Come from the sea with breadth of approaching brightness.
When the blithe wind laughs on the hills with uplifted voice.

When I'm Among a Blaze of Lights . . .

When I'm among a blaze of lights,
With tawdry music and cigars
And women dawdling through delights,
And officers at cocktail bars, —
Sometimes I think of garden nights
And elm trees nodding at the stars.

I dream of a small firelit room
With yellow candles burning straight.
And glowing pictures in the gloom,
And kindly books that hold me late.
Of things like these I love to think
When I can never be alone:
Then someone says, "Another drink?" —
And turns my living heart to stone.

Golgotha

Through darkness curves a spume of falling flares
That flood the field with shallow, blanching light.
        The huddled sentry stares
        On gloom at war with white,
        And white receding slow, submerged in gloom.
        Guns into mimic thunder burst and boom.
        And mirthless laughter rakes the whistling night.
The sentry keeps his watch where no one stirs
But the brown rats, the nimble scavengers.

A Mystic as Soldier

I lived my days apart,
Dreaming fair songs for God,
By the glory in my heart
Covered and crowned and shod.

Now God is in the strife.
And I must seek Him there,
Where death outnumbers life,
And fury smites the air.

I walk the secret way
With anger in my brain.
O music through my clay.
When will you sound again?

The Kiss

To these I turn, in these I trust;
Brother Lead and Sister Steel.
To his blind power I make appeal;
I guard her beauty clean from rust.

He spins and burns and loves the air,
And splits a skull to win my praise;
But up the nobly marching days
She glitters naked, cold and fair.

Sweet Sister, grant your soldier this;
That in good fury he may feel
The body where he sets his heel
Quail from your downward darting kiss.

The Redeemer

Darkness: the rain sluiced down; the mire was deep;
It was past twelve on a mid-winter night,
When peaceful folk in beds lay snug asleep:
There, with much work to do before the light,
We lugged our clay-sucked boots as best we might

Along the trench; sometimes a bullet sang.
And droning shells burst with a hollow bang;
We were soaked, chilled and wretched, every one.
Darkness: the distant wink of a huge gun.

I turned in the black ditch, loathing the storm;
A rocket fizzed and burned with blanching flare.
And lit the face of what had been a form
Floundering in mirk. He stood before me there;
I say that he was Christ; stiff in the glare,
And leaning forward from his burdening task,
Both arms supporting it; his eyes on mine
Stared from the woeful head that seemed a mask
Of mortal pain in Hell's unholy shine.

No thorny crown, only a woollen cap
He wore — an English soldier, white and strong,
Who loved his time like any simple chap.
Good days of work and sport and homely song;
Now he has learned that nights are very long.
And dawn a watching of the windowed sky.
But to the end, unjudging, he'll endure
Horror and pain, not uncontent to die
That Lancaster on Lune may stand secure.

He faced me, reeling in his weariness.
Shouldering his load of planks, so hard to bear.
I say that he was Christ, who wrought to bless
All groping things with freedom bright as air,
And with His mercy washed and made them fair

Then the flame sank, and all grew black as pitch,
While we began to struggle along the ditch;
And someone flung his burden in the muck.
Mumbling: "O Christ Almighty, now I'm stuck

A Subaltern

He turned to me with his kind, sleepy gaze
And fresh face slowly brightening to the grin
That sets my memory back to summer days
With twenty runs to make, and last man in.
He told me he'd been having a bloody time
In trenches, crouching for the "crumps" to burst,
While squeaking rats scampered across the slime
And the grey palsied weather did its worst.

But as he stamped and shivered in the rain.
My stale philosophies had served him well;
Dreaming about his girl had sent his brain
Blanker than ever — she'd no place in Hell. . . .
"Good God!" he laughed, and calmly filled his pipe,
Wondering "why he always talked such tripe."

"In the Pink"

So Davies wrote: " This leaves me in the pink."
Then scrawled his name: *' Your loving sweetheart, Willie."
With crosses for a hug. He'd had a drink
Of rum and tea; and, though the barn was chilly.
For once his blood ran warm; he had pay to spend.
Winter was passing; soon the year would mend.

He couldn't sleep that night. Stiff in the dark
He groaned and thought of Sundays at the farm,
When he'd go out as cheerful as a lark
In his best suit to wander arm-in-arm
With brown-eyed Gwen, and whisper in her ear
The simple, silly things she liked to hear.

And then he thought: to-morrow night we trudge
Up to the trenches, and my boots are rotten.
Five miles of stodgy clay and freezing sludge,
And everything but wretchedness forgotten.
To-night he's in the pink; but soon he'll die.
And still the war goes on; he don't know why.

A Working Party

Three hours ago he blundered up the trench,
Sliding and poising, groping with his boots;
Sometimes he tripped and lurched against the walls
With hands that pawed the sodden bags of chalk.
He couldn't see the man who walked in front;
Only he heard the drum and rattle of feet
Stepping along the trench-boards, — often splashing
Wretchedly where the sludge was ankle-deep.

Voices would grunt, " Keep to your right, — make way!
When squeezing past the men from the front-line:
White faces peered, puffing a point of red;

Candles and braziers glinted through the chinks
And curtain-flaps of dug-outs; then the gloom
Swallowed his sense of sight; he stooped and swore
Because a sagging wire had caught his neck.
A flare went up; the shining whiteness spread
And flickered upward, showing nimble rats,
And mounds of glimmering sand-bags, bleached with rain;

Then the slow, silver moment died in dark.
The wind came posting by with chilly gusts
And buffeting at corners, piping thin
And dreary through the crannies; rifle-shots
Would split and crack and sing along the night.
And shells came calmly through the drizzling air
To burst with hollow bang below the hill.

Three hours ago he stumbled up the trench;
Now he will never walk that road again:
He must be carried back, a jolting lump
Beyond all need of tenderness and care;
A nine-stone corpse with nothing more to do.

He was a young man with a meagre wife
And two pale children in a Midland town;
He showed the photograph to all his mates;
And they considered him a decent chap
Who did his work and hadn't much to say.
And always laughed at other people's jokes
Because he hadn't any of his own.

That night, when he was busy at his job
Of piling bags along the parapet,
He thought how slow time went, stamping his feet,
And blowing on his fingers, pinched with cold.
He thought of getting back by half-past twelve.
And tot of rum to send him warm to sleep
In draughty dug-out frowsty with the fumes
Of coke, and full of snoring, weary men.

He pushed another bag along the top.
Craning his body outward; then a flare
Gave one white glimpse of No Man's Land and wire;
And as he dropped his head the instant split
His startled life with lead, and all went out.

A Whispered Tale

I'd heard fool-heroes brag of where they'd been,
With stories of the glories that they'd seen,
Till there was nothing left for shame to screen.

But you, good, simple soldier, seasoned well
In woods and posts and crater-lines of hell,
Who dodge remembered "crumps" with wry grimace, —
Cold hours of torment in your queer, kind face,
Smashed bodies in your strained, unhappy eyes,
And both your brothers killed to make you wise;
Vou had no empty babble; what you said
Was like a whisper from the maimed and dead.
But Memory brought the voice I knew, whose note
Was smothered when they shot you in the throat;
And still you whisper of the war, and find
Sour jokes for all those horrors left behind.

"Blighters"

The House is crammed: tier beyond tier they grin
And cackle at the Show, while prancing ranks
Of harlots shrill the chorus, drunk with din;
"We're sure the Kaiser loves the dear old Tanks!"

I'd like to see a Tank come down the stalls,
Lurching to rag-time tunes, or "Home, sweet Home," —
And there'd be no more jokes in Music-halls
To mock the riddled corpses round Bapaume.

At Carnoy

Down in the hollow there's the whole Brigade
Camped in four groups: through twilight falling slow
I hear a sound of mouth-organs, ill-played,
And murmur of voices, gruff, confused, and low.
Crouched among thistle-tufts I've watched the glow
Of a blurred orange sunset flare and fade;
And I'm content. To-morrow we must go
To take some cursed Wood. . . O world God made!

July 3rd, 1916.

To His Dead Body

When roaring gloom surged inward and you cried,
Groping for friendly hands, and clutched, and died.
Like racing smoke, swift from your lolling head
Phantoms of thought and memory thinned and fled.

Yet, though my dreams that throng the darkened stair
Can bring me no report of how you fare,
Safe quit of wars, I speed you on your way
Up lonely, glimmering fields to find new day,
Slow-rising, saintless, confident and kind —
Dear, red-faced father God who lit your mind.

Two Hundred Years After

Trudging by Corbie Ridge one winter's night,
(Unless old, hearsay memories tricked his sight).
Along the pallid edge of the quiet sky
He watched a nosing lorry grinding on.
And straggling files of men; when these were gone,
A double limber and six mules went by,
Hauling the rations up through ruts and mud
To trench-lines digged two hundred years ago.
Then darkness hid them with a rainy scud,
And soon he saw the village lights below.

But when he'd told his tale, an old man said
That he'd seen soldiers pass along that hill;
"Poor, silent things, they were the English dead
"Who came to fight in France and got their fill."

"They"

The Bishop tells us: "When the boys come back
"They will not be the same; for they'll have fought
"In a just cause: they lead the last attack
"On Anti-Christ; their comrade's blood has bought
"New right to breed an honourable race.
"They have challenged Death and dared him face to face."

"We're none of us the same!" the boys reply.
"For George lost both his legs; and Bill's stone blind;
"Poor Jim's shot through the lungs and like to die;
"And Bert's gone siphilitic: you'll not find
"A chap who's served that hasn't found some change."
And the Bishop said: "The ways of God are strange!"

Stand-to: Good Friday Morning

I'd been on duty from two till four.
I went and stared at the dug-out door.
Down in the frowst I heard them snore.
  "Stand to!" Somebody grunted and swore.
  Dawn was misty; the skies were still;
  Larks were singing, discordant, shrill;
  They seemed happy; but I felt ill.
Deep in water I splashed my way
Up the trench to our bogged front line.
Rain had fallen the whole damned night.
O Jesus, send me a wound to-day.
And I'll believe in Your bread and wine,
And get my bloody old sins washed white!

Special-Constable

"Put out that light!" he cried.
But no one put it out.
No one replied.
And silence gulped his husky shout.

Against the door he blundered.
Knocked — but no one came.
Wrathful, he wondered;
"What's their number? What's their name? "

And the moon above the town
Through wisps of cloud looked down
On roofs and cowls
And cats and constables and owls.

He clutched his truncheon tight,
For he was bold that night.
And hurled it high
Up at the lit and lawless sky.

He bawled: "Then go to Hell!"
And, reeling home to bed,
Blue brilliance fell
From moons that danced within his head.

The Choral Union

He staggered in from night and frost and fog,
And lampless streets: he'd guzzled like a hog,
And drunk till he was dazed; and now he came
To hear he couldn't call to mind the name, —
But he'd been given a ticket for the show,
And thought he'd (hiccup) chance his luck and go.

The hall swam in his eyes, and soaring light
Was dazzling-splendid after the dank night.
He sat and blinked, safe in his cushioned seat,
And licked his lips; he'd like a brandy, neat.

"Who is the King of Glory?" they were saying —
He pricked his ears; what was it? Were they praying? . . . .
By God, it might be Heaven! For singers stood
Ranked in pure white; and everyone seemed good;

And clergymen were sitting meekly round
With joyful faces, drinking in the sound;
And holy women, and plump, whiskered men.
Could this be Heaven? And was he dead? . . . . and then
They all stood up; the mighty chorus broke
In storms of song above those blameless folk;
And "Hallelujah, Hallelujah!" rang
The burden of the triumph that they sang.

He gasped; it must be true; he'd got to Heaven
With all his sins that seventy times were seven;
And whispering "Hallelujah," mid their shout,
He wondered when Lord God would turn him out.

Liquor-Control

[To Roderick Meiklejohn]

In the time of the war with the Philistine,

Solomon uttered a law that said:
"Down with the Sign of the Saracen's Head,
"Shut up the Star and the Sun and the Vine!"

Then the King went in to his glimmering dames
And called the roll of their languorous names;
But the Moon-faced Lily, the pearl divine,
Swooned and implored, and was sick for wine.

Down in the harem something stirred,
But none of the eunuchs whispered a word.
Glug, glug, glug! the concubines poured
Warm wet liquor in health to their lord.

And Solomon spoke in a drunken voice:
"Let cymbals sound! Let the people rejoice!"
So the Jew-boys looked on the wine that was red
In the Vine and the Star and the Saracen's Head.

The One-Legged Man

Propped on a stick he viewed the August weald;
Squat orchard trees and oasts with painted cowls;
A homely, tangled hedge, a corn-stooked field,
With sound of barking dogs and farmyard fowls.

And he'd come home again to find it more
Desirable than ever it was before.
How right it seemed that he should reach the span
Of comfortable years allowed to man!

Splendid to eat and sleep and choose a wife,
Safe with his wound, a citizen of life.
He hobbled blithely through the garden gate,
And thought: "Thank God they had to amputate!"

Enemies

He stood alone in some queer sunless place
Where Armageddon ends; perhaps he longed
For days he might have lived; but his young face
Gazed forth untroubled: and suddenly there thronged
Round him the hulking Germans that I shot
When for his death my brooding rage was hot.

He stared at them, half-wondering; and then
They told him how I'd killed them for his sake, —
Those patient, stupid, sullen ghosts of men:
And still there seemed no answer he could make.
At last he turned and smiled, and all was well
Because his face could lead them out of hell.

The Tombstone-Maker

He primmed his loose red mouth, and leaned his head
Against a sorrowing angel's breast, and said:
"You'd think so much bereavement would have made
"Unusual big demands upon my trade.
"The War comes cruel hard on some poor folk —
"Unless the fighting stops I'll soon be broke."

He eyed the Cemetery across the road —
"There's scores of bodies out abroad, this while,
"That should be here by rights; they little know'd
"How they'd get buried in such wretched style."

I told him, with a sympathetic grin.
That Germans boil dead soldiers down for fat;
And he was horrified. "What shameful sin!
"O sir, that Christian men should come to that!"

Arms and the Man

Young Croesus went to pay his call
On Colonel Sawbones, Caxton Hall:
And, though his wound was healed and mended.
He hoped he'd get his leave extended.

The waiting-room was dark and bare.
He eyed a neat-framed notice there
Above the fireplace hung to show
Disabled heroes where to go
For arms and legs; with scale of price,
And words of dignified advice
How officers could get them free.

Elbow or shoulder, hip or knee, —
Two arms, two legs, though all were lost.

They'd be restored him free of cost.

Then a Girl-Guide looked in to say,
"Will Captain Croesus come this way?"

Died of Wounds

His wet, white face and miserable eyes
Brought nurses to him more than groans and sighs:
But hoarse and low and rapid rose and fell
His troubled voice: he did the business well.

The ward grew dark; but he was still complaining,
And calling out for "Dickie." "Curse the Wood!
"It's time to go , O Christ, and what's the good? —
"We'll never take it; and it's always raining."

I wondered where he'd been; then heard him shout,
"They snipe like hell! O Dickie, don't go out "...
I fell asleep . . . next morning he was dead;
And some Slight Wound lay smiling on his bed.

The Hero

"Jack fell as he'd have wished," the Mother said,
And folded up the letter that she'd read.
"The Colonel writes so nicely." Something broke
In the tired voice that quavered to a choke.
She half looked up. "We mothers are so proud
"Of our dead soldiers." Then her face was bowed.

Quietly the Brother Officer went out.
He'd told the poor old dear some gallant lies
That she would nourish all her days, no doubt.
For while he coughed and mumbled, her weak eyes
Had shone with gentle triumph, brimmed with joy,
Because he'd been so brave, her glorious boy.

He thought how "Jack," cold-footed, useless swine,
Had panicked down the trench that night the mine
Went up at Wicked Corner; how he'd tried
To get sent home; and how, at last, he died.
Blown to small bits. And no one seemed to care
Except that lonely woman with white hair.

Stretcher Case

[To Edward Marsh]

He woke: the clank and racket of the train
Kept time with angry throbbings in his brain.
Then for a while he lapsed and drowsed again.

At last he lifted his bewildered eyes
And blinked, and rolled them sidelong; hills and skies,
Heavily wooded, hot with August haze.
And, slipping backward, golden for his gaze.
Acres of harvest.

                    Feebly now he drags
Exhausted ego back from glooms and quags
And blasting tumult, terror, hurtling glare,
To calm and brightness, havens of sweet air.

He sighed, confused; then drew a cautious breath;
This level journeying was no ride through death.
"If I were dead," he mused, "there'd be no thinking —
"Only some plunging underworld of sinking,
"And hueless, shifting welter where I'd drown."

Then he remembered that his name was Brown.

But was he back in Blighty? Slow he turned,
Till in his heart thanksgiving leapt and burned.
There shone the blue serene, the prosperous land.
Trees, cows and hedges; skipping these, he scanned
Large, friendly names that change not with the year,
Lung Tonic, Mustard, Liver Pills and Beer.

Conscripts

"Fall in, that awkward squad, and strike no more
"Attractive attitudes! Dress by the right!
"The luminous rich colours that you wore
"Have changed to hueless khaki in the night.
"Magic? What's magic got to do with you?
"There's no such thing! Blood's red and skies are blue."

They gasped and sweated, marching up and down.
I drilled them till they cursed my raucous shout.
Love chucked his lute away and dropped his crown.
Rhyme got sore heels and wanted to fall out.
"Left, right! Press on your butts!" They looked at me
Reproachful; how I longed to set them free!

I gave them lectures on Defence, Attack;
They fidgeted and shuffled, yawned and sighed,
And boggled at my questions. Joy was slack,
And Wisdom gnawed his fingers, gloomy-eyed.
Young Fancy — how I loved him all the while —
Stared at his note-book with a rueful smile.

Their training done, I shipped them all to France.
Where most of those I'd loved too well got killed.
Rapture and pale Enchantment and Romance,
And many a sickly, slender lord who'd filled
My soul long since with lutanies of sin.
Went home, because they couldn't stand the din.

But the kind, common ones that I despised,
(Hardly a man of them I'd count as friend),
What stubborn-hearted virtues they disguised!
They stood and played the hero to the end,
Won gold and silver medals bright with bars.
And marched resplendent home with crowns and stars.

The Road

The road is thronged with women; soldiers pass
And halt, but never see them; yet they're here —
A patient crowd along the sodden grass.
Silent, worn out with waiting, sick with fear.
The road goes crawling up a long hillside.
All ruts and stones and sludge, and the emptied dregs
Of battle thrown in heaps. Here where they died
Are stretched big-bellied horses with stiff legs;
And dead men, bloody-fingered from the fight.
Stare up at caverned darkness winking white.

You in the bomb-scorched kilt, poor sprawling Jock,
You tottered here and fell, and stumbled on,
Half dazed for want of sleep. No dream could mock
Your reeling brain with comforts lost and gone.
You did not feel her arms about your knees,

Her blind caress, her lips upon your head:
Too tired for thoughts of home and love and ease,
The road would serve you well enough for bed.

Secret Music

I keep such music in my brain
No din this side of death can quell, —
Glory exulting over pain,
And beauty, garlanded in hell.

My dreaming spirit will not heed
The roar of guns that would destroy
My life that on the gloom can read
Proud-surging melodies of joy.

To the world's end I went, and found
Death in his carnival of glare;
But in my anguish I was crowned,
And music dawned above despair.

Nimrod in September

When half the drowsy world's a-bed
And misty morning rises red,
With jollity of horn and lusty cheer,
Young Nimrod urges on his dwindling rout;
Along the yellowing coverts we can hear
His horse's hoofs thud hither and about:
In mulberry coat he rides and makes
Huge clamour in the sultry brakes.

Morning Express

Along the wind-swept platform, pinched and white,
The travellers stand in pools of wintry light,
Offering themselves to morn's long, slanting arrows.
The train's due; porters trundle laden barrows.
The train steams in, volleying resplendent clouds
Of sun-blown vapour. Hither and about,
Scared people hurry, storming the doors in crowds.
The officials seem to waken with a shout.

Resolved to hoist and plunder; some to the vans
Leap; others rumble the milk in gleaming cans.

Boys, indolent-eyed, from baskets leaning back,
Question each face; a man with a hammer steals
Stooping from coach to coach; with clang and clack.
Touches and tests, and listens to the wheels.
Guard sounds a warning whistle, points to the clock
With brandished flag, and on his folded flock
Claps the last door: the monster grunts; "Enough!
Tightening his load of links with pant and puff.
Under the arch, then forth into blue day.
Glide the processional windows on their way,
And glimpse the stately folk who sit at ease
To view the world like kings taking the seas
In prosperous weather: drifting banners tell
Their progress to the counties; with them goes
The clamour of their journeying; while those
Who sped them stand to wave a last farewell.

Noah

When old Noah started across the floods
Sky and water melted into one
Looking-glass of shifting tides and sun.

Mountain-tops were few: the ship was foul:
All the morn old Noah marvelled greatly
At this weltering world that shone so stately,
Drowning deep the rivers and the plains.
Through the stillness came a rippling breeze;
Noah sighed, remembering the green trees.

Clear along the morning stooped a bird, —
Lit beside him with a blossomed sprig.
Earth was saved; and Noah danced a jig.

Policeman

Sitting in the hedge I hear
Through sunlit morning fresh and still
Sounds and voices far and near,
And sheep-bells under the green hill.
Who's a-trudging up the lane?

Whistling birds around him saying;
"Spring, spring, you're here again!
"April's come, and lambs are playing!"

Policeman's eye says: "Who are you?"
Pacing past me stiff and slow,
Tightly buttoned up in blue,
Hot and stately. And I know
If I jump down, and in my fun
Clout his red ear, then start to run,
He'll grab me quick and give me hell,
And lock me up in quod as well.

David Cleek

I cannot think that Death will press his claim
To snuff you out or put you off your game:
You'll still contrive to play your steady round,
Though hurricanes may sweep the dismal ground.
And darkness blur the sandy-skirted green
Where silence gulfs the shot you strike so clean.

Saint Andrew guard your ghost, old David Cleek,
And send you home to Fifeshire once a week!
Good-fortune speed your ball upon its way
When Heaven decrees its mightiest Medal-Day:
Till crowds of Angels chant for evermore
The miracle of your unbeaten score;
And He who keeps all players in His sight.
Walking the royal and ancient hills of light.
Standing benignant at the eighteenth hole.
To everlasting Golf consigns your soul.

Ancestors

Behold these jewelled, merchant Ancestors,
Foregathered in some chancellery of death;
Calm, provident, discreet, they stroke their beards
And move their faces slowly in the gloom.
And barter monstrous wealth with speech subdued,
Lustreless eyes and acquiescent lids.
        And oft in pauses of their conference,
        They listen to the measured breath of night's
        Hushed sweep of wind aloft the swaying trees

In dimly gesturing gardens; then a voice
Climbs with clear mortal song half-sad for heaven.

A silent-footed message flits and brings
The ghostly Sultan from his glimmering halls;
A shadow at the window, turbaned, vast,
He leans; and, pondering the sweet influence
That steals around him in remembered flowers,
Hears the frail music wind along the slopes.
Put forth, and fade across the whispering sea.

Haunted

Evening was in the wood, louring with storm.
A time of drought had sucked the weedy pool
And baked the channels; birds had done with song.
Thirst was a dream of fountains in the moon,
Or willow-music blown across the water
Leisurely sliding on by weir and mill.

Uneasy was the man who wandered, brooding.
His face a little whiter than the dusk.
A drone of sultry wings flicker'd in his head.

The end of sunset burning thro' the boughs
Died in a smear of red; exhausted hours
Cumber'd, and ugly sorrows hemmed him in.

He thought: "Somewhere there's thunder," as he strove
To shake off dread; he dared not look behind him.
But stood, the sweat of horror on his face.

He blundered down a path, trampling on thistles.
In sudden race to leave the ghostly trees.
And: " Soon I'll be in open fields," he thought,
And half remembered starlight on the meadows,
Scent of mown grass and voices of tired men,
Fading along the field-paths; home and sleep
And cool-swept upland spaces, whispering leaves,
And far off the long churring night-jar's note.

But something in the wood, trying to daunt him.
Led him confused in circles through the brake.
He was forgetting his old wretched folly,
And freedom was his need; his throat was choking;
Barbed brambles gripped and clawed him round his legs.

And he floundered over snags and hidden stumps.
Mumbling: "I will get out! I must get out!"
Butting and thrusting up the baffling gloom.
Pausing to listen in a space 'twixt thorns,
He peers around with boding, frantic eyes.
An evil creature in the twilight looping.
Flapped blindly in his face. Beating it off,
He screeched in terror, and straightway something clambered
Heavily from an oak, and dropped, bent double,
To shamble at him zigzag, squat and bestial.

Headlong he charges down the wood, and falls
With roaring brain — agony — the snap't spark —
And blots of green and purple in his eyes.
Then the slow fingers groping on his neck,
And at his heart the strangling clasp of death.

Blind

His headstrong thoughts that once in eager strife
Leapt sure from eye to brain and back to eye,
Weaving unconscious tapestries of life,
Are now thrust inward, dungeoned from the sky.
And he who has watched his world and loved it all,
Starless and old and blind, a sight for pity.
With feeble steps and fingers on the wall.
Gropes with his staff along the rumbling city.

Before Day

Come in this hour to set my spirit free
When earth is no more mine though night goes out
And stretching forth these arms I cannot be
Lord of winged sunrise and dim Arcady:
When fieldward boys far off with clack and shout
From orchards scare the birds in sudden rout.
Come, ere my heart grows cold and full of doubt
In the still summer dawns that waken me.

When the first lark goes up to look for day,
And morning glimmers out of dreams, come then,
Out of the songless valleys, over gray
Wide misty lands to bring me on my way:

For I am lone, a dweller among men.
Hungered for what my heart shall never say.

Villon

They threw me from the gates: my matted hair
Was dank with dungeon wetness; my spent frame
O'erlaid with marish agues: everywhere
Tortured by leaping pangs of frost and flame,
I was so hideous that even Lazarus there
In noisome rags arrayed and leprous shame,
Beside me set had seemed full sweet and fair.
And looked on me with loathing. But one came
Who wrapped me in his cloak and bore me in
Tenderly to an hostel quiet and clean, —
Used me with healing hands for all my needs.
The foul estate of my unshriven sin,
My long disgrace, and loveless, lecherous deeds,
He has put by as though they had not been.

Goblin Revel

In gold and grey, with fleering looks of sin,
I watch them come; by two, by three, by four,
Advancing slow, with loutings they begin
Their woven measure widening from the door;
While music-men behind are straddling in
With flutes to brisk their feet across the floor, —
And jangled dulcimers, and fiddles thin
That taunt the twirling antic through once more.

They pause, and hushed to whispers, steal away
With cunning glances; silent go their shoon
Upon the stairs: but far away the dogs
Bark at some lonely farm; and haply they
Have clambered back into the dusky moon
That sinks beyond the marshes loud with frogs.

Night-Piece

Ye hooded witches, baleful shapes that moan.
Quench your fantastic lanterns and be still;

For now the moon through heaven sails alone,
Shedding her peaceful rays from hill to hill.
The faun from out his dim and secret place
Draws nigh the darkling pool and from his dream
Half-wakens, seeing there his sylvan face
Reflected, and the wistful eyes that gleam.

To his cold lips he sets the pipe to blow
Some drowsy note that charms the listening air:
The dryads from their trees come down and creep
Near to his side; monotonous and low.
He plays and plays till all the woodside there
Stirs to the voice of everlasting sleep.

A Wanderer

[To Hamo Thornycroft]

When Watkin shifts the burden of his cares
And all that irked him in his dull employ,
Once more become a vagrom-hearted boy,
He moves to roundelays and jocund airs:
Afield with lusty harvestmen he shares
Old ale and sunshine; or, with maids half-coy
Pays court to shadows; clowns himself with joy.
And shakes a leg at junketings and fairs.

Sometimes, returning down his breezy miles,
A snatch of wayward April he will bring,
Piping the daffodilly that beguiles
Foolhardy lovers in the surge of spring:
And then once more by lanes and field-path stiles
Up the green world he wanders like a king.

October

Across the land a faint blue veil of mist
Seems hung; the woods wear yet arrayment sober,
Till frost shall make them flame; silent and whist
The drooping cherry orchards of October
Like mournful pennons hang their shrivelling leaves
Russet and orange: all things now decay;
Long since ye garnered in your autumn sheaves.
And sad the robins pipe at set of day.

Now do ye dream of Spring when greening shaws
Confer with the shrewd breezes, and of slopes
Flower-kirtled, and of April, sweetling guest;
Days that ye love, despite their windy flaws,
Since they are woven with all joys and hopes
Whereof ye nevermore shall be possessed.

The Heritage

Cry out on Time that he may take away
Your cold philosophies that give no hint
Of spirit-quickened flesh; fall down and pray
That Death come never with a face of flint.
Death is our heritage; with Life we share
The sunlight that must own his darkening hour;
Within his very presence yet we dare
To gather gladness like a fading flower.

For even as this, our joy not long may live
Perfect; and most in change the heart can trace
The miracle of life and human things.
All we have held, to destiny we give;
Dawn glimmers on the soul-forsaken face;
Not we, but others, hear the bird that sings.

An Old French Poet

When in your sober mood my body ye have laid
In sight and sound of things beloved, woodland and stream,
And the green turf has hidden the poor bones ye deem
No more a close companion with those rhymes we made;

Then, if some bird should pipe, or breezes stir the glade,
Thinking them for the while my voice, so let them seem
A fading message from the misty shores of dream.
Or wheresoever, following Death, my feet have strayed.

Dryads

When meadows are grey with the morn,
In the dusk of the woods it is night;

The oak and the ash and the pine
War with the glimmer of light.

Dryads brown as the leaf
Move in the gloom of the glade;
When meadows are grey with the morn.
Dim night in the wood has delayed.

The cocks that crow to the land
Are faint and hollow and shrill:
Dryads as brown as the leaf
Whisper and hide and are still.

Before the Battle

Music of whispering trees
Hushed by the broad-winged breeze
Where shaken water gleams;
And evening radiance falling
With reedy bird-notes calling.
O bear me safe through dark, you low-voiced streams

I have no need to pray
That fear may pass away;
I scorn the growl and rumble of the fight
That summons me from cool
Silence of marsh and pool,
And yellow lilies islanded in light.
O river of stars and shadows, lead me through the night.

June 25th 1916.

Morning-Land

Old English songs, you bring to me
A simple sweetness somewhat kin
To birds that through the mystery
Of earliest morn made tuneful din,
While hamlet steeples sleepily
At cock-crow chime out three and four.
Till maids get up betime and go,
With faces like the red sun low,
Clattering about the dairy floor.

Arcady Unheeding

Shepherds go whistling on their way
In the green glory of the year;
One watches weather-signs of day;
One of his maid most dear
Dreams; and they do not hear
The birds that sing and sing; they do not see
Wide wealds of blue beyond their windy lea,
Nor blossoms red and white on every tree.

Gibbet

You that in moonlit meadows wander,
See where your lover waits you yonder.
Who has no guineas now to squander.

There stands the lad your eyes were seeking,
Whose absence made your false heart fonder —
His limbs in rusty fetters creaking.

The yellow moon shines clear above him:
Go sit with him; he'll ne'er forsake you:
Hie to him quick and say you love him.
And hear what answer he will make you.

Dream Forest

Where sunshine flecks the green,
Through towering woods my way
Goes winding all the day.
Scant are the flowers that bloom
Beneath the bosky screen
And cage of golden gloom.
Few are the birds that call,
Shrill-voiced and seldom seen.

Where silence masters all.
And light my footsteps fall,
The whispering runnels only
With blazing noon confer;
And comes no breeze to stir

The tangled thickets lonely.

A Child's Prayer

For Morn, my dome of blue,
For Meadows, green and gay,
And Birds who love the twilight of the leaves.
Let Jesus keep me joyful when I pray.

For the big Bees that hum
And hide in bells of flowers;
For the winding roads that come
To Evening's holy door,
May Jesus bring me grateful to his arms.
And guard my innocence for evermore.

Morning Glory

In this meadow starred with spring
Shepherds kneel before their king.
Mary throned, with dreaming eyes,
Gowned in blue like rain-washed skies.
Lifts her tiny son that he
May behold their courtesy.
And green-smocked children, awed and good,
Bring him blossoms from the wood.

Clear the sunlit steeples chime
Mary's coronation-time.
Loud the happy children quire
To the golden-windowed morn;
While the lord of their desire
Sleeps below the crimson thorn.

To-day

This is To-day, a child in white and blue
Running to meet me out of Night who stilled
The ghost of Yester-eve; this is fair Morn
The mother of To-morrow. And these clouds
That chase the sunshine over gleaming hills
Are thoughts, delighting in the golden change

And the ceremony of their drifting state.

This is To-day. To-morrow might bring death, —
And Life, the gleeful madrigal of birds,
Be drowned in glimmer of sleep. To-day I know
How sweet it is to spend these eyes, and boast
This bubble of vistaed memory and sense
Blown by my joy aloft the glittering airs
Of heavenly peace. Oh take me to yourselves.
Earth, sky, and spirit! Let me stand within
The circle of your transience, that my voice
May thrill the lonely silences with song.

Wonderment

Then a wind blew;
And he, who had forgot he moved
Lonely amid the green and silver morning weather.
Suddenly grew
Aware of clouds and trees
Gleaming and white and shafted, shaken together
And blown to music by the ruffling breeze.

Like flush of wings
The moment passed: he stood
Dazzled with blossom in the swaying wood;
Then he remembered how, through all swift things.
This mortal scene stands built of memories, —
Shaped by the wise
Who gazed in breathing wonderment,
And left us their brave eyes
To light the ways they went.

Daybreak in a Garden

I heard the farm cocks crowing, loud, and faint, and thin.
When hooded night was going and one clear planet winked:
I heard shrill notes begin down the spired wood distinct,
When cloudy shoals were chinked and gilt with fires of day.
White-misted was the weald; the lawns were silver-grey;
The lark his lonely field for heaven had forsaken;
And the wind upon its way whispered the boughs of may.
And touched the nodding peony-flowers to bid them waken.

Companions

Leave not your bough, my slender song-bird sweet.
But pipe me now your roundelay complete.

Come, gentle breeze, and tarrying on your way.
Whisper my trees what you have seen to-day.

Stand, golden cloud, until my song be done,
(For he's too proud), before the face of the sun.

So one did sing, and the other breathed a story;
Then both took wing, and the sun stepped forth in glory.

A Poplar and the Moon

There stood a Poplar, tall and straight;
The fair, round Moon, uprisen late,
Made the long shadow on the grass
A ghostly bridge 'twixt heaven and me.
        But May, with slumbrous nights, must pass;
        And blustering winds will strip the tree.
And I've no magic to express
The moment of that loveliness;
So from these words you'll never guess
The stars and lilies I could see.

South Wind

Where have you been, South Wind, this May-day morning.
With larks aloft, or skimming with the swallow.
Or with blackbirds in a green, sun-glinted thicket?

Oh, I heard you like a tyrant in the valley;
Your ruffian haste shook the young, blossoming orchards;
You clapped rude hands, hallooing round the chimney.
And white your pennons streamed along the river.

You have robbed the bee, South Wind, in your adventure.
Blustering with gentle flowers; but I forgave you
When you stole to me shyly with scent of hawthorn.

Tree and Sky

Let my soul, a shining tree,
Silver branches lift towards thee.
Where on a hallowed winter's night
The clear-eyed angels may alight.

And if there should be tempests in
My spirit, let them surge like din
Of noble melodies at war;

With fervour of such blades of triumph as are
Flashed in white orisons of saints who go
On shafts of glory to the ecstasies they know.

Alone

I've listened: and all the sounds I heard
Were music, — wind, and stream, and bird.
With youth who sang from hill to hill
I've listened: my heart is hungry still.

I've looked: the morning world was green;
Bright roofs and towers of town I've seen.
And stars, wheeling through wingless night.
I've looked: and my soul yet longs for light.

I've thought: but in my sense survives
Only the impulse of those lives
That were my making. Hear me say,
"I've thought!" — and darkness hides my day.

Storm and Sunlight

I

In barns we crouch, and under stacks of straw,
Harking the storm that rides a hurtling legion
Up the arched sky, and speeds quick heels of panic
With growling thunder loosed in fork and clap
That echoes crashing thro' the slumbrous vault.
The whispering woodlands darken: vulture Gloom

Stoops, menacing the skeltering flocks of Light,
Where the gaunt shepherd shakes his gleaming staff
And foots with angry tidings down the slope.
Drip, drip; the rain steals in through soaking thatch
By cob-webbed rafters to the dusty floor.
Drums shatter in the tumult; wrathful Chaos
Points pealing din to the zenith, then resolves
Terror in wonderment with rich collapse.

II.

Now from drenched eaves a swallow darts to skim
The crystal stillness of an air unveiled
To tremulous blue. Raise your bowed heads, and let
Your horns adorn the sky, ye patient kine!
Haste, flashing brooks! Small, chuckling rills, rejoice!
Be open-eyed for Heaven, ye pools of peace!
Shine, rainbow hills! Dream on, fair glimpsed vale
In haze of drifting gold! And all sweet birds,
Sing out your raptures to the radiant leaves!
And ye, close huddling Men, come forth to stand
A moment simple in the gaze of God
That sweeps along your pastures! Breath his might!
Lift your blind faces to be filled with day,
And share his benediction with the flowers.

Wind in the Beechwood

The glorying forest shakes and swings with glancing
Of boughs that dip and strain; young, slanting sprays
Beckon and shift like lissom creatures dancing,
While the blown beechwood streams with drifting rays.

Rooted in steadfast calm, grey stems are seen
Like weather-beaten masts; the wood, unfurled
Seems as a ship with crowding sails of green,
That sweep across the lonely, billowing world.

O luminous and lovely! Let your flowers,
Your ageless-squadroned wings, your surge and gleam,
Drown me in quivering brightness: let me fade
In the warm, rustling music of the hours
That guard your ancient wisdom, till my dream
Moves with the chant and whisper of the glade.

Wisdom

When Wisdom tells me that the world's a speck
Lost on the shoreless blue of God's To-Day. . .
I smile, and think, " For every man his way:
"The world's my ship, and I'm alone on deck!"

But when he tells me that the world's a spark
Lit in the whistling gloom of God's To-Night. . .
I look within me to the edge of dark.
And dream, "The world's my field, and I'm the lark,
"Alone with upward song, alone with light!"

The Death-Bed

He drowsed and was aware of silence heaped
Round him, unshaken as the steadfast walls;
Aqueous like floating rays of amber light.
Soaring and quivering in the wings of sleep, —
Silence and safety; and his mortal shore
Lipped by the inward, moonless waves of death.

Someone was holding water to his mouth.
He swallowed, unresisting; moaned and dropped
Through crimson gloom to darkness; and forgot
The opiate throb and ache that was his wound.
Water — calm, sliding green above the weir;
Water — a sky-lit alley for his boat.
Bird-voiced, and bordered with reflected flowers
And shaken hues of summer: drifting down.
He dipped contented oars, and sighed, and slept.

Night, with a gust of wind, was in the ward,
Blowing the curtain to a glimmering curve.
Night. He was blind; he could not see the stars
Glinting among the wraiths of wandering cloud;
Queer blots of colour, purple, scarlet, green,
Flickered and faded in his drowning eyes.

Rain; he could hear it rustling through the dark;
Fragrance and passionless music woven as one;
Warm rain on drooping roses; pattering showers
That soak the woods; not the harsh rain that sweeps
Behind the thunder, but a trickling peace

Gently and slowly washing life away.

He stirred, shifting his body; then the pain
Leaped like a prowling beast, and gripped and tore
His groping dreams with grinding claws and fangs.
But someone was beside him; soon he lay
Shuddering because that evil thing had passed.
And death, who'd stepped toward him, paused and stared.

Light many lamps and gather round his bed.
Lend him your eyes, warm blood, and will to live.
Speak to him; rouse him; you may save him yet.
He's young; he hated war; how should he die
When cruel old campaigners win safe through?

But Death replied: "I choose him." So he went,
And there was silence in the summer night;
Silence and safety; and the veils of sleep.
Then, far away, the thudding of the guns.

The Last Meeting

I.

Because the night was falling warm and still
Upon a golden day at April's end,
I thought; I will go up the hill once more
To find the face of him that I have lost,
And speak with him before his ghost has flown
Far from the earth that might not keep him long.

So down the road I went, pausing to see
How slow the dusk drew on, and how the folk
Loitered about their doorways, well-content
With the fine weather and the waxing year.
The miller's house, that glimmered with grey walls.
Turned me aside; and for a while I leaned
Along the tottering rail beside the bridge
To watch the dripping mill-wheel green with damp.

The miller peered at me with shadowed eyes
And pallid face: I could not hear his voice
For the insistent water. He was old:
His days went round with the unhurrying wheel.

Moving along the street, each side I saw

The humble, kindly folk in lamp-lit rooms;
Children at table; simple, homely wives;
Strong, grizzled men; and soldiers back from war.
Scaring the gaping elders with loud talk.

Soon all the jumbled roofs were down the hill,
And I was turning up the grassy lane
That goes to the big, empty house that stands
Above the town, half-hid by towering trees.
I looked below and saw the glinting lights:
I heard the treble cries of bustling life.
And mirth, and scolding; and the grind of wheels.
An engine whistled, piercing-shrill, and called
High echoes from the sombre slopes afar;
Then a long line of trucks began to move.

It was quite still; the columned chestnuts stood
Dark in their noble canopies of leaves.
I thought: "A little longer I'll delay,
"And then he'll be more glad to hear my feet,
"And with low laughter ask me why I'm late.
"The place will be too dim to show his eyes;
"But he will loom above me like a tree,
"With lifted arms and body tall and strong."

There stood the empty house; a ghostly hulk
Becalmed and huge, massed in the mantling dark.
As builders left it when quick-shattering war
Leapt upon France and called her men to fight.
Lightly along the terraces I trod,
Crunching the rubble till I found the door
That gaped in twilight, framing inward gloom.
An owl flew out from under the high eaves
To vanish secretly among the firs,
Where lofty boughs netted the gleam of stars.
I stumbled in; the dusty floors were strewn
With cumbering piles of planks and props and beams;
Tall windows gapped the walls; the place was free
To every searching gust and jousting gale;
But now they slept: I was afraid to speak,
And heavily the shadows crowded in.

I called him, once; then listened: nothing moved:
Only my thumping beat out the time.
Whispering his name, I groped from room to room.

Quite empty was that house; it could not hold
His human ghost, remembered in the love

That strove in vain to be companioned still.

II.

Blindly I sought the woods that I had known
So beautiful with morning when I came
Amazed with spring that wove the hazel copse
With misty raiment of awakening green.
I found a holy dimness, and the peace
Of sanctuary, austerely built of trees,
And wonder stooping from the tranquil sky.

Ah! but there was no need to call his name.
He was beside me now, as swift as light.
I knew him crushed to earth in scentless flowers.
And lifted in the rapture of dark pines.
"For now," he said, "my spirit has more eyes
"Than heaven has stars; and they are lit by love.
My body is the magic of the world.
And dawn and sunset flame with my spilt blood.
My breath is the great wind, and I am filled
With molten power and surge of the bright waves
That chant my doom along the ocean's edge.

"Look in the faces of the flowers and find
The innocence that shrives me; stoop to the stream
That you may share the wisdom of my peace.
For talking water travels undismayed.
The luminous willows lean to it with tales
Of the young earth; and swallows dip their wings
Where showering hawthorn strews the lanes of light.

"I can remember summer in one thought
Of wind-swept green, and deeps of melting blue,
And scent of limes in bloom; and I can hear
Distinct the early mower in the grass,
Whetting his blade along some morn of June.

"For I was born to the round world's delight,
And knowledge of enfolding motherhood,
Whose tenderness, that shines through constant toil,
Gathers the naked children to her knees.
In death I can remember how she came
To kiss me while I slept; still I can share
The glee of childhood; and the fleeting gloom
When all my flowers were washed with rain of tears.

"I triumph in the choruses of birds.
Bursting like April buds in gyres of song,
My meditations are the blaze of noon
On silent woods where glory burns the leaves.
I have shared breathless vigils; I have slaked
The thirst of my desires in bounteous rain
Pouring and splashing downward through the dark.
Loud storm has roused me with its winking glare,
And voice of doom that crackles overhead.
I have been tired and watchful, craving rest,
Till the slow-footed hours have touched my brows
And laid me on the breast of sundering sleep."

III.

I know that he is lost among the stars,
And may return no more but in their light.
Though his hushed voice may call me in the stir
Of whispering trees I shall not understand.
Men may not speak with stillness; and the joy
Of brooks that leap and tumble down green hills
Is faster than their feet; and all their songs
Can win no meaning from the talk of birds.

My heart is fooled with fancies, being wise;
For fancy is the gleaming of wet flowers
When the hid sun looks forth with golden stare.
Thus, when I find new loveliness to praise,
And things long-known shine out in sudden grace,
Then will I think: "He moves before me now."
So he will never come but in delight;
And, as it was in life, his name shall be
Wonder awaking in a summer dawn,
And youth, that dying, touched my lips to song.

A Letter Home

[To Robert Graves]

I.

Here I'm sitting in the gloom
Of my quiet attic room.
France goes rolling all around,
Fledged with forest May has crowned.

And I puff my pipe, calm-hearted.
Thinking how the fighting started.
Wondering when we'll ever end it.
Back to Hell with Kaiser send it.
Gag the noise, pack up and go,
Clockwork soldiers in a row.
I've got better things to do
Than to waste my time on you.

II.

Robert, when I drowse to-night.
Skirting lawns of sleep to chase
Shifting dreams in mazy light,
Somewhere then I'll see your face
Turning back to bid me follow
Where I wag my arms and hollo,
Over hedges hasting after
Crooked smile and baffling laughter,
Running tireless, floating, leaping,
Down your web-hung woods and valleys.
Garden glooms and hornbeam alleys.
Where the glowworm stars are peeping.
Till I find you, quiet as stone
On a hill-top all alone.
Staring outward, gravely pondering
Jumbled leagues of hillock-wandering.

III.

You and I have walked together
In the starving winter weather.
We've been glad because we knew
Time's too short and friends are few,
We've been sad because we missed
One whose yellow head was kissed
By the gods, who thought about him
Till they couldn't do without him.
Now he's here again; I've seen
Soldier David dressed in green,
Standing in a wood that swings
To the madrigal he sings.
He's come back, all mirth and glory,
Like the prince in a fairy story.
Winter called him far away;
Blossoms bring him home with May.

IV.

Well, I know you'll swear it's true
That you found him decked in blue
Striding up through morning-land
With a cloud on either hand.
Out in Wales, you'll say, he marches
Arm-in-arm with oaks and larches;
Hides all night in hilly nooks,
Laughs at dawn in tumbling brooks.
Yet, it's certain, here he teaches
Outpost-schemes to groups of beeches.
And I'm sure, as here I stand,
That he shines through every land.
That he sings in every place
Where we're thinking of his face.

V.

Robert, there's a war in France;
Everywhere men bang and blunder.
Sweat and swear and worship Chance,
Creep and blink through cannon thunder.
Rifles crack and bullets flick.
Sing and hum like hornet-swarms.
Bones are smashed and buried quick.
Yet, through stunning battle storms.
All the while I watch the spark
Lit to guide me; for I know
Dreams will triumph, through the dark
Scowls above me where I go.
Ton can hear me; you can mingle
Radiant folly with my jingle.
War's a joke for me and you
While we know such dreams are true!

Siegfried Sassoon – A Short Biography

Siegfried Loraine Sassoon was born on 8th September 1886. He grew up in the neo-gothic mansion 'Weirleigh', in Matfield, Kent.

His father, Alfred Ezra Sassoon, was a member of the wealthy Baghdadi Jewish Sassoon merchant family. For marrying outside the faith he was disinherited. His mother, Theresa, was from the Anglo-Catholic

Thornycroft family, the sculptors responsible for many of the best-known statues in London. Interestingly she named him Siegfried because of her love for Wagner's operas rather than any German ancestry. He was the second of three sons. When he was four years old his parents separated.

Sassoon was educated at the New Beacon School, Sevenoaks, Kent then Marlborough College, Wiltshire and finally at Clare College, Cambridge, where from 1905 to 1907 he read history. He went down from Cambridge without a degree and spent the next few years indulging himself hunting, playing cricket and writing verse: some of which he published privately. Sassoon had only a small private income that, provided he lived modestly, negated the need to work, though in later years he would be left a generous legacy by his aunt, Rachel Beer, allowing him to buy the estate of Heytesbury House in Wiltshire.

His first published success, 'The Daffodil Murderer' (1913), was a parody of John Masefield's 'The Everlasting Mercy'. His great friend Robert Graves describes it as a "parody of Masefield which, midway through, had forgotten to be a parody and turned into rather good Masefield."

Sassoon was a good amateur cricketer and was keen to play for Kent County Cricket Club. He often turned out for the Bluemantles, where he sometimes played alongside another keen cricketer, Arthur Conan Doyle. Although an enthusiast, Sassoon was not good enough to play for Kent, but he continued to play cricket into his seventies.

Sassoon had proffered his opinions on the political situation before the First World War thus—"France was a lady, Russia was a bear, and performing in the county cricket team was much more important than either of them".

However, motivated by patriotism, Sassoon joined the British Army as the threat of war escalated. He was in service with the Sussex Yeomanry on 4th August 1914, the day war was declared on Germany.

He broke his arm badly in a riding accident and was therefore out of action before even leaving England. He spent the spring of 1915 convalescing. Sassoon was commissioned into the 3rd Battalion (Special Reserve), Royal Welch Fusiliers, as a second lieutenant on 29th May 1915. On 1st November his younger brother Hamo was killed in the Gallipoli Campaign, and that same month Sassoon was sent to the 1st Battalion in France. There he met Robert Graves, and they became close friends, drawn together by their poetic ambitions, they would read and discuss each other's work. Graves' views on what may be called 'gritty realism' profoundly affected Sassoon's idea of what poetry was. Life on the front line meant he soon became horrified by the slaughter and daily realities of war, and the tone of his writing changed dramatically: where his early poems exhibit a Romantic, dilettantish sweetness, his war poetry moves to an increasingly discordant beat, stridently conveying the ugly truths of the trenches to an audience hitherto placated by jingoistic and patriotic propaganda.

Conversely Sassoon's periods of duty on the Western Front were marked by exceptionally brave actions, including the single-handed capture of a German trench in the Hindenburg Line. Armed with grenades, he scattered sixty German soldiers.

Sassoon's bravery was so inspiring that his fellow soldiers said they felt confident only when they were accompanied by him. He often went out on night-raids and bombing patrols and demonstrated ruthless efficiency as a company commander. Deepening depression at the horror and misery the soldiers were forced to endure produced in Sassoon a paradoxically manic courage, and earned him the nickname

'Mad Jack' by his men for his many and near-suicidal exploits. On 27th July 1916 Sassoon was awarded the Military Cross. He was also later recommended for the Victoria Cross.

His poetry both described the horrors of the trenches and satirised the patriotic pretensions of those who, in Sassoon's view, were responsible for a jingoism-fuelled war.

Despite his decorations and reputation, in 1917 Sassoon decided to make a stand against the running of the war. At the end of a spell of convalescent leave, Sassoon declined to return to duty; instead, encouraged by pacifist friends such as Bertrand Russell and Lady Ottoline Morrell, he sent a letter to his commanding officer entitled 'Finished with the War: A Soldier's Declaration'. Forwarded to the press and read out in the House of Commons by a sympathetic member of Parliament, the letter was seen by some as treasonous ('I am making this statement as an act of wilful defiance of military authority') and by others as condemning the war government's motives ('I believe that the war upon which I entered as a war of defence and liberation has now become a war of aggression and conquest'). Rather than court-martial Sassoon, the authorities decided that he was unfit for service and had him sent to Craiglockhart War Hospital near Edinburgh. This facility had opened in 1916 as a military psychiatric hospital to care for officers suffering from the psychological effects of the Great War, such as neurasthenia ('shell shock').

At Craiglockhart, Sassoon met Wilfred Owen, a poet who would eventually exceed him in fame. It was perhaps thanks to Sassoon that Owen persevered in his ambition to write better poetry. Both men returned to active service in France. Owen would later be killed in 1918, just a week before Armistice. Sassoon, despite all this, was promoted to lieutenant, and having spent some time away from danger in Palestine, eventually returned to the front line.

On 13th July 1918, Sassoon was almost immediately wounded again—by friendly fire when he was shot in the head by a British soldier who had mistaken him for a German near Arras, France. As a result, he spent the remaining months of the war in Britain. By this time he had been promoted to acting captain.

On 12th March 1919 Sassoon relinquished his commission on health grounds but was allowed to retain the rank of captain.

He now dabbled briefly in the politics of the Labour movement which was now gathering strength after the first two tumultuous decades of the 20th Century.

In 1919 took up a post as literary editor of the socialist Daily Herald. Here he was responsible for employing several eminent names as reviewers, including E. M. Forster and Charlotte Mew. Sassoon also commissioned new material from the likes of Arnold Bennett and Osbert Sitwell. He also managed to now extend his own interests to include music.

Sassoon now accepted a lecture tour of the United States and travelled throughout Europe and across Britain. He came into possession of a car, a gift from the publisher Frankie Schuster. He became renowned among his friends for his poor driving skills, which apparently did not discourage him from making full use of the car.

In 1923 he visited Wales. Sassoon was a great admirer of the Welsh poet Henry Vaughan and paid a pilgrimage to his grave at Llansantffraed, Powys. It was there he wrote one of his best-known peacetime poems, 'At the Grave of Henry Vaughan'.

Unhappily there came the deaths in quick succession of three of his closest friends; Edmund Gosse, Thomas Hardy and Frankie Schuster, causing a serious setback to his personal happiness.

Sassoon was now, in 1928, preparing to take a new direction by branching out into prose, with 'Memoirs of a Fox-Hunting Man'. This anonymously published first volume of a fictionalised autobiography, was acclaimed as a classic, bringing its author fame as a humorous writer. The book won the 1928 James Tait Black Award for fiction. Sassoon followed it with 'Memoirs of an Infantry Officer' (1930) and 'Sherston's Progress' (1936). Some time later he would write his own autobiography based on his youth and early manhood across three volumes, which were also widely acclaimed. These were 'The Old Century', 'The Weald of Youth' and 'Siegfried's Journey'.

Sassoon, having matured greatly as a result of his military service, continued to seek long-lasting, loving relationships. Initially these were with a succession of men.

In September 1931, Sassoon rented Fitz House, Teffont Magna, Wiltshire and began to live there. In December 1933, he married Hester Gatty, who was many years his junior. The marriage led to the birth of a child, George, which he had craved for a long time.

By 1945 Sassoon was separated from his wife and was living in seclusion at Heytesbury in Wiltshire, although he continued to keep contact with a circle which included E.M. Forster and J.R. Ackerley. One of his closest friends was the cricketer, Dennis Silk who would become Warden (headmaster) of Radley College. He also formed a close friendship with Vivien Hancock, the headmistress of Greenways School at Ashton Gifford, where his son George was a pupil. This provoked Hester to make strong accusations against her who then responded with a threat of legal action.

In his last years Sassoon converted to Roman Catholicism. He had hoped that Ronald Knox, a Roman Catholic priest and writer whom he admired, would instruct him in the faith, but Knox was too ill to take on the task. The priest Sebastian Moore was chosen to instruct him instead, and Sassoon was admitted to the faith at Downside Abbey in Somerset. He also paid regular visits to the nuns at Stanbrook Abbey, and their press printed commemorative editions of some of his poems.

Sassoon was appointed Commander of the Order of the British Empire (CBE) in the 1951 New Year Honours.

Siegfried Loraine Sassoon, CBE, MC died from stomach cancer on 1st September 1967, a week before his 81st birthday. He is buried at St Andrew's Church, Mells, Somerset.

On 11th November 1985, Sassoon was among sixteen Great War poets commemorated on a slate stone unveiled in Westminster Abbey's Poet's Corner. The inscription on the stone was written by friend and fellow War poet Wilfred Owen. It reads: "My subject is War, and the pity of War. The Poetry is in the pity."

Siegried Sassoon – A Concise Bibliography

Poetry

The Daffodil Murderer (1913)
The Old Huntsman and Other Poems (1917)
Counter-Attack and Other Poems (1918)
The War Poems of Siegfried Sassoon (1919)
Picture-Show (1919)
Recreations (1923)
Lingual Exercises for Advanced Vocabularians (1925)
Selected Poems (1925)
Satirical Poems (1926)
The Heart's Journey (1928)
Poems by Pinchbeck Lyre (1931)
The Road to Ruin (1933)
Vigils (1935)
Rhymed Ruminations (1940)
Poems Newly Selected (1940)
Collected Poems (1947)
Common Chords (1950/1951)
Emblems of Experience (1951)
The Tasking (1954)
Sequences (1956)
Lenten Illuminations (1959)
The Path to Peace (1960)
Collected Poems 1908-1956 (1961)
The War Poems ed. Rupert Hart-Davis (1983)

Prose

Memoirs of a Fox-Hunting Man (1928)
Memoirs of an Infantry Officer (1930)
Sherston's Progress (1936)
Complete Memoirs of George Sherston (1937)
The Old Century (1938)
On Poetry (1939)
The Weald of Youth (1942)
Siegfried's Journey (1945)
Meredith (1948)

Other Works

Finished with the War: A Soldier's Declaration (1917)
"Introduction" to Poems by Wilfred Owen (1920)

www.ingramcontent.com/pod-product-compliance
Lightning Source LLC
Chambersburg PA
CBHW021944040426
42448CB00008B/1235